WARTIME BROADCASTING

Mike Brown

Shire Publications, an imprint of Osprey Publishing Ltd
c/o Bloomsbury Publishing Plc
PO Box 883, Oxford, OX1 9PL, UK

Or

c/o Bloomsbury Publishing Inc.
1385 Broadway, 5th Floor, New York, NY 10018,
USA

E-mail: shire@bloomsbury.com

www.shirebooks.co.uk

SHIRE is a trademark of Osprey Publishing Ltd, a
division of Bloomsbury Publishing Plc.

First published in Great Britain in 2018

A CIP catalogue record for this book is available from
the British Library.

Shire Library no. 845.

ISBN: PB: 978 1 78442 264 6

          ePub: 978 1 78442 262 2

          ePDF: 978 1 78442 261 5

          XML: 978 1 78442 263 9

18 19 20 21 22   10 9 8 7 6 5 4 3 2 1

Mike Brown has asserted his right under the
Copyright, Designs and Patents Act, 1988, to be
identified as the author of this book.

Typeset in Garamond Pro and Gill Sans

Page layouts by PDQ Digital Media Solutions,
Bungay, UK

Printed in China through World Print Ltd.

COVER IMAGE
Front cover: Detail of the front of an old Philips radio
(Alamy). Back cover: The government was worried
that BBC buildings might be taken over by German
paratroopers or fifth columnists. BBC workers were
issued with this special war service badge.

TITLE PAGE IMAGE
In the late 1930s, while television was available, it was
extremely expensive; for most people the wireless was
their daily form of home entertainment, information,
and news.

CONTENTS PAGE IMAGE
Murphy Radio advertisement from 1940 – 'munitions
for the home front'. The wireless would prove
an invaluable vehicle for news, information and
instructions, as well as in keeping up morale.

ACKNOWLEDGEMENTS
The photos on pages 25, 26, 37 (top) and 55 are
Crown Copyright; those on pages 4, 7, 35 and 39 are
from Getty Images. All other photographs, illustrations
and artefacts are from the author's collection.

Shire Publications is supporting the Woodland Trust, the UK's leading woodland conservation charity, by funding the dedication of trees.

CONTENTS

EARLY DAYS

IT SEEMS STRANGE to think that in 1939 the BBC was relatively new, having been formed as a private company in 1922, and only becoming the national corporation in 1927. It had grown quickly: in 1938 nearly nine million wireless licences were issued.

After the Munich crisis that September, when Britain and France were very nearly plunged into war with Germany, the BBC began preparing for what many saw as an inevitable war.

There were those in government, Chamberlain among them, who believed that wireless broadcasting – or at least the entertainment side – should cease in the event of war, leaving it a vehicle for government advice, instructions, and news. These functions were vital to the conduct of war, meaning the BBC also would be vital. It was therefore crucial that bombing should not disrupt its output through knocked-out broadcasting studios or masts. This would not only break a vital link between the government and the people, but also create confusion and panic. Another challenge was to avoid enemy aircraft being able to use radio transmissions as a homing beam.

It was decided that the solution to both these problems was, in the event of war, to merge the BBC National and Regional Programmes into a single channel – the Home Service – broadcast throughout the country. Programmes would be produced at several locations, limiting the damage to the system that would occur if one were knocked out.

Comedian and singer Arthur Askey, along with 'Dicky' Murdoch, had been a great hit before the war with their show 'Band Waggon', returning to the airwaves in mid-September 1939.

In the event, Broadcasting House was hit twice, but the BBC was never forced off the air.

With that possibility in mind, however, in 1938 the BBC made plans in case London had to be evacuated. Wood Norton Hall, a Victorian stately home near Evesham, was secretly bought and equipped in the months before war broke out. Although never used in its emergency role, by 1940 Wood Norton was one of the largest broadcasting centres in Europe with an average output of 1,300 programmes a week. It also became the BBC's monitoring service centre until early 1943, when monitoring moved to Reading, so that Wood Norton could become the main broadcasting centre if London had to be evacuated due to the V-weapon assault.

Further provision was made at Bristol, where the BBC prepared an underground fortress beneath fifty feet of solid sandstone in a disused funicular railway tunnel driven through the Clifton gorge in the 1890s. The BBC took it over to convert it to an air raid shelter for Sir Adrian Boult's BBC Symphony Orchestra, which had been evacuated nearby with the Music Department. However, in 1941 in the face of bombing raids, the Music Department moved to Bedford, and the tunnel became the nerve centre of the BBC in the West of England. The roof of the tunnel was waterproofed, and electric lighting installed. In three months four large chambers were built and outfitted, sending programmes in about forty different languages all over the world.

On 24 August 1939, during the last uneasy days of peace, the BBC demonstrated its value in a crisis, when it was used to

summon teachers back from their summer holidays to prepare for evacuation.

Just before dawn on 1 September, German forces invaded Poland – an act that would propel Britain into war. The BBC was immediately placed on a war footing, the first act of which would be the closure of the infant BBC television service that lunchtime – it would not return until after the war. That evening the plan to unify the BBC wireless channels was put into effect, the changeover being announced to the listening public at 6pm.

Robert MacDermott later recalled:

For nearly two hours on that evening I sat alone in a studio at Broadcasting House, playing through an immense pile of records and informing listeners every three minutes that at 8.15p.m. the National and Regional programmes would cease to exist, to be replaced by a single programme, the Home Service.

Tommy Handley (right), whose programme, 'It's That Man Again', first appeared in July 1939. With him are 'ITMA' stalwarts Jack Train (Colonel Chinstrap), and Dorothy Summers (Mrs Mopp).

He was alone because most of his colleagues had left – the second act of the BBC's war preparations. In his book, *ITMA 1939–1948* Francis Worsley described the situation:

> For some weeks before war was declared we in the B.B.C. were under, as it were, sealed orders. As at that time a tremendous bombing attack on London was expected immediately after the outbreak of hostilities, elaborate plans were made for immediate evacuation of London and dispersal of the various programme departments to various provincial centres, so that a broadcasting service could be kept going if the raids paralysed the capital.

The Drama Department moved to Evesham, the Music and Variety Departments to Bristol, and the Religious Department to Bedford.

The first task on arrival was to find suitable premises for conversion into studios. Parish halls proved most suitable; stone structures with slated timber roofs and wood on joist floors provided just the right amount of reverberation. Modern buildings, especially those constructed of concrete, were generally unsatisfactory and were rejected. The problem of absorbing middle and high notes was tackled by hanging absorbing material from the walls and ceiling, and carpeting the floor. This became known as 'the BBC's washing'.

The deadline for German troop withdrawal ran out at 11am on 3 September. Robert Wood was in charge of the BBC team at Downing Street, waiting to broadcast Chamberlain's words to the world. He wrote:

> We were just waiting, because Chamberlain was waiting – for some message from somewhere to say that Hitler was going to reply. But Hitler said nothing. Minutes ticked by and the Prime Minister still hesitated. At Broadcasting House tension was high and I was on edge too. The

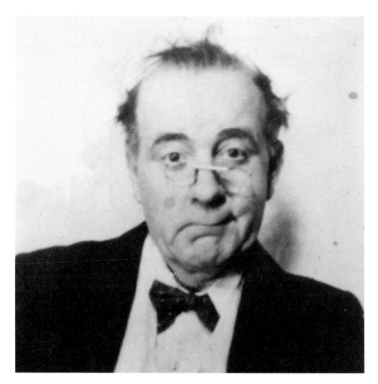

Comedian Robb Wilton appeared frequently on the BBC throughout the war as bumbling JP Mr Muddlecombe, or giving one of his monologues, which often started, 'The day war broke out...'.

Cabinet by this time were standing like wax figures and still Chamberlain sat, pale-faced and silent before the microphones. The time was 11.15 and finally I said to him, 'Sir, the world is waiting.'

He looked at me and replied, 'Well then, we'll make the announcement now.'

It is a sign of the effectiveness of the BBC that the vast majority of the population heard that the country was at war on the 'wireless'. Chamberlain's speech began:

I am speaking to you from the Cabinet Room at 10 Downing Street. This morning the British Ambassador in Berlin handed the German government a final note stating that unless we heard from them by 11 o'clock that

Sandy MacPherson. The Canadian organist was one of the few live acts on the Home Service during the first days of war, most of the acts having been evacuated.

they were prepared at once to withdraw their troops from Poland, a state of war would exist between us. I have to tell you now that no such undertaking has been received, and that consequently this country is at war with Germany.

After this the national anthem was played; then long lists of government announcements and advice to the public were read out, such as to carry their gas masks, what to do in an air raid, and so on. There followed a day of news bulletins every hour, interspersed with official notices, instructions, regulations and exhortations.

Between these were programmes of gramophone recordings. Due to the exodus of large numbers of BBC staff to their new billets in the country, there remained only a skeleton staff at Portland Place. For the first few days virtually the only live music was Sandy MacPherson at the organ. As the BBC put it, he 'played the theatre organ for you till his feet were numb and his fingers nearly dropped off. You appreciated his efforts but were by no means appeased.' Many were far less generous.

At 6pm on 3 September, King George VI broadcast the following message from Buckingham Palace:

In this grave hour, perhaps the most fateful in our history, I send to every household of my peoples, both at home and overseas, this message, spoken with the same depth of feeling for each one of you as if I were able to cross your threshold and speak to you myself.

The *Radio Times* of 4 September 1939, with its 'revised programmes for Sept. 4–10'. These changes in programming were due to the outbreak of war, the creation of the Home Service, and the evacuation of BBC staff.

One of the programmes added to the new schedule for the first week of the war was, rather ominously, 'First Steps in First Aid', broadcast on Monday 4 September.

FIRST STEPS in
FIRST AID

This evening at 6.25 a well-known London doctor will give the first of a series of practical talks on things you should know about First Aid. He speaks again on Tuesday, Wednesday, Thursday, Friday and Saturday

(See diagrams on page 5)

… I now call my people at home and my peoples across the seas, who will make our cause their own. I ask them to stand calm, firm, and united in this time of trial. The task will be hard. There may be dark days ahead, and war can no longer be confined to the battlefield. But we can only do the right as we see the right, and reverently commit our cause to God.

If one and all we keep resolutely faithful to it, ready for whatever service or sacrifice it may demand, then, with God's help, we shall prevail.

The *Radio Times* rushed out a new issue with revised programmes for 4–10 September. Everything was geared to a short but violent conflict, with hourly news bulletins designed to keep the public up to date with a fast-changing conflict. However, contrary to the expected air raids in Britain, and fighting on the Maginot line, the public were faced with what the American press dubbed 'the phoney war'. The news bulletins tried hard to bulk out what was happening, but people soon grew frustrated with the lack of hard news. The wireless, it seemed, had become an official bully, haranguing the public with directions and regulations, but no news.

Within three days, in spite of the extraordinary difficulties of the changeover, on Wednesday, 6 September the first live revue of the war, 'Songs from the Shows', was broadcast from the Variety Department's new headquarters in Bristol. 'Children's Hour', which had been cancelled for the first two days of the war, was also back, though cut down to half an hour.

On 16 September 'Band Waggon', the smash hit of the year, had its first wartime airing, and three days later came the first 'It's That Man Again' of the war, though not yet under its wartime name. During that first month of the war, 118 live shows were broadcast, thanks largely to two orchestras and a scratch repertory company of twenty-two.

The war the BBC and the authorities had planned for had not materialised; both had to reappraise their plans given the breathing space the lack of action brought. It would not, of course, last, but when action did come, the BBC was far better prepared.

Derek McCulloch, or 'Uncle Mac' to fans of 'Children's Hour'. After the first few days of war programmes reverted to something like normal and 'Children's Hour' was back.

RADIO FUN

3

No. 26
Oct. 30
1943

EVERY THURSDA

BIG-HEARTED ARTHUR and DICKY MURDOCH

HELLO ALL! VIC OLIVER CALLING ON THE RADIO FUN WAVE-LENGTH
"I call my maid Dawn—you know why, perhaps!"
"It's 'cause she's always breaking, gels and chaps!"

ENTERTAINMENT

IN THE FIRST days of war a new 'Variety Centre' was set up in Bristol, but with the start of serious bombing, Bristol came under increasing air assault. In April 1941, Variety moved to Bangor, and by autumn 1943 they were back in London. The Music Department, including the BBC Symphony Orchestra and Sir Adrian Boult, had also moved to Bristol, but relocated to Bedford in September 1941, joining the Religious Department already there.

With only one channel, it was imperative to hold on to the audience. This meant broadcasting popular programmes; to achieve this the BBC carried out intensive research into what people listened to and what they thought about it. Established favourites such as 'Band Waggon' and 'It's That Man Again' were on the bill, but new programmes could be hit-and-miss, and there were those within the BBC and beyond who thought people should be provided with what they *needed*, rather than what they wanted.

'Popular' in 1939 meant variety, especially light music and comedy. One of the early programmes of the war, 'Band Waggon', supplied both. Started in January 1938, it portrayed the adventures of Arthur Askey and Richard 'Stinker' Murdoch in their imaginary flat above Broadcasting House. 'It's That Man Again', which had first appeared in July 1939, re-appeared in September of that year. Undoubtedly the most popular programme of the war, 'ITMA' (as its wartime audience soon knew it) starred Tommy Handley

OPPOSITE:
Radio Fun comic, October 1943. Stories included Our Brains Trust, the Western Brothers, Bebe Daniels and Ben Lyon, Tommy Handley and Funf, Flanagan and Allen, Jack Warner and Vic Oliver.

'ITMA' postcards, each carrying one of its character's catchphrases: left, Mrs Mopp; right, Colonel Chinstrap. These catchphrases became common currency during the war.

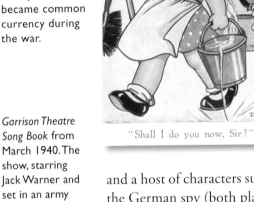

"Shall I do you now, Sir?"

WE DON'T MIND

PRE WAR

IF WE DO!

WITH APOLOGIES TO ITMA

Garrison Theatre Song Book from March 1940. The show, starring Jack Warner and set in an army camp theatre, was one of the early hits of the war.

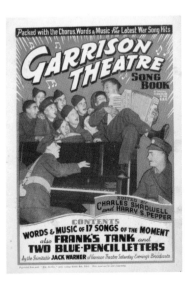

and a host of characters such as Colonel Chinstrap and Funf, the German spy (both played by Jack Train). Each character had their own catchphrases, and before long, people across the country were saying, 'I don't mind if I do', 'This is Funf speaking', and 'after You Claude', 'No, after you, Cecil.' Handley's irreverent take on officialdom – he was the 'Minister of Aggravation and Mysteries' or from 'the Office of Twerps' – struck a chord, especially at a time of increasing bureaucracy.

There was a new series each autumn, with new situations, characters, and catchphrases, including in 1941, Mrs Mopp (Dorothy Summers) – 'Shall I do you now, sir?'

The first new hit of the war, broadcast from November 1939, was 'Garrison Theatre', a version of the revues used to entertain the troops. Compered by Jack Warner, its raucous music-hall atmosphere was aided by lively audiences of service men and women. A 1940 hit was 'Hi, Gang!' with its three stars, Americans Ben Lyon and Bebe Daniels, and Vic Oliver.

The following year saw 'Happidrome' with Ramsbottom, and Enoch and me (Robbie Vincent, Cecil Fredericks and Harry Korris), the 'Old Town Hall', 'Old Mother Riley takes the Air' (starring Arthur Lucan and Kitty McShane), and probably the most unlikely hit of the war, 'The Brains Trust'.

On 1 January 1941, 'Any Questions?' appeared in the Forces Programme. Designed as a general knowledge programme, 'serious in intention, light in character', it comprised five experts discussing questions collected from members of the forces about philosophy, art, and science, and was concerned more with them demonstrating their knowledge, or lack of it, rather than an attempt to spread knowledge. Donald McCullough put the questions to the panel, made up of regulars Professor Julian Huxley, 'Professor' Cyril Joad, Commander A.B. Campbell, and two guests. Howard Thomas nicknamed the panel 'the brains trust', and the name stuck, becoming the title in 1942. It was a massive success, attracting a regular audience of at least ten million. In its wake sprang up dozens of army, rotary, and village 'brains trusts'.

By 1941, the Variety Department was producing around 180 shows a week performed by the Variety Repertory Company, the BBC Dance Band, the Revue and Variety

The Brains Trust Book. The show, based on a panel of academics answering obscure questions of fact or philosophy, was one of the most unexpected hits of the Second World War.

The Brains Trust in person (from left to right): Philip Guedalla, Professor Julian Huxley, Ritchie Calder, C.E.M. Joad, Commander Campbell, and the 'question master', D.S. McCullough.

Orchestras, but not the BBC theatre organ. The instrument played throughout the first days of the war by Sandy MacPherson had been destroyed by enemy action.

By this time seven to ten plays a week were being broadcast; of these, 90 per cent came from the BBC repertory company. A regular series, 'Saturday Night Theatre', started that April, and was intended to provide popular plays for 'the average listener'. *Barchester Towers* and *The Woman in White* provided radio serials, while listeners were invited to a weekly 'Appointment with Fear', often introduced by Valentine Dyall, 'the man in black'.

In 1943 came an eight-part dramatisation of *War and Peace*, and a production of *Peer Gynt*, with Ralph Richardson in the title role. John Gielgud starred in *Pilgrim's Progress*, music for which was specially composed by Vaughan Williams and played by the BBC Orchestra.

Heavy bombing in Bristol meant that many of the Music Department's programmes had to be pre-recorded to ensure freedom from interruption. With the move to Bedford in September 1941, it became possible to broadcast almost all Home Service music programmes 'live'.

Sir Adrian Boult, appointed the BBC's first Director of Music in 1930, and conductor of the BBC Symphony Orchestra, in an advertisement from the *Gramophone* magazine of October 1944.

Henry Hall. Before the war, he had been the leader of the BBC Dance Band, but left to form his own dance band, with which he broadcast regularly during the war.

The introduction of the Forces Programme in February 1940 increased the time available for musical broadcasts of all types, especially light and comparatively light music, while the time available on the Home Service was often used for more serious music, symphony concerts on Wednesday evenings and Sunday afternoons forming the most important orchestral broadcasts of the week. There were also dance-band broadcasts, including the 'BBC Dancing Club' and 'Radio Rhythm Club'.

Besides its symphony orchestra, the BBC had its own theatre orchestra, salon orchestra, and military band, as well as its choir, the BBC Chorus.

With the military setbacks of 1942 came criticism of the service. A few very vociferous people argued that sentimental songs and singers had a demoralising effect on the troops, calling

HENRY HALL

for a ban on 'sloppy' lyrics, male crooners, and overly sentimental female singers. The BBC gave way. At the same time the American forces were beginning to arrive. They were completely under-awed by the BBC's output, and demanded, and in 1943 got, their own station, the 'American Forces Network'. Many British listeners also tuned in. Again, there followed much huffing and puffing, but eventually, popular programmes won.

On 23 June 1940, the BBC began an experimental series of programmes called 'Music While You Work', a daily ration

Leaflet for the Dictograph factory loudspeaker system from June 1940, which states, 'The BBC yesterday inaugurated a twice-weekly broadcast of music for munition and factory workers – 'Music while you work'.'

Small concert parties (ENSA) began putting on shows for troops – these spread to cover factories, becoming 'Workers' Playtime'. Here, George Formby entertains factory workers in their canteen.

of music during the morning and afternoon, which made the hours pass more quickly and resulted in greatly increased worker productivity.

The BBC carried out research among workers to discover their preferences, and among factories to establish their needs. The most satisfactory music was found to be light rhythmical dance music with a clear melodic line. One result of the research was the decision to exclude vocal items, which, reports showed, acted as a distraction unless the words were well known. However, if music went on all day it lost its effect; half an hour, mid-morning and mid-afternoon

WORKERS' PLAYTIME

'Workers' Playtime' postcard from 1944. Bands and comics would perform in factory canteens and the resulting show was broadcast across the country.

when boredom is greatest, had the best results. The result was the morning and afternoon programme 'Music while you work', reaching, in 1940–41, around 750,000 people.

On 2 August 1942, a third session at half-past ten in the evening was introduced for night-shift workers. Bands included theatre orchestras, light orchestras, military bands, brass bands, and dance bands. Its audience continued to grow, and by 1944 over 8,000 factories, covering more than 4.5 million workers, received the programmes daily.

The next stage was to bring shows to the factories, and to broadcast the result. This became 'Workers' Playtime'. With the blessing of the Ministry of Labour, the first broadcast took place in May 1941.

A small temporary wooden stage would be erected at one end of the factory canteen, the microphone slung from the roof, and the entertainment given to as many workers as could be packed into the available space, with the broadcast relayed throughout the whole works and on the BBC, so that everybody could hear it. 'Workers' Playtime' was broadcast live twice, then three times a week at lunchtime. During 1942 broadcasts were given from factories, dockyards, and a shipbuilding yard. In September, the show was even performed to agricultural workers from a stage set up in a field and decorated with harvest produce. In July, 'Workers' Playtime' was joined by 'Break for Music', factory concerts from ENSA (Entertainments National Service Association), broadcast by the BBC.

Meanwhile in 1941, the workers themselves provided the talent in shows such as 'Factory Canteen' until 1942, and 'Works Wonders', the latter carrying on until 1951.

After the first few days of confusion, 'Children's Hour' was back on air from 6 September 1939, its pre-war sixty minutes reduced to forty. Old favourites continued to flourish, such as 'Toy Town' and broadcasts by the 'Zoo Man' (David Seth-Smith) and 'Romany'.

There were war-related items: 'Uncle Mac' and Lieutenant-Colonel O'Gorman spoke of the need for young listeners to obey the rule of 'safety first' on the roads. Commander King-Hall, another old favourite, spoke on fuel economy, and children were encouraged to gather rose hips and collect salvage; there was even a special gas-mask drill, by John Snagge.

'THE ANCIENT MARINER'.
Coleridge's famous poem is the theme of a programme for schools this afternoon at 2.35.

Advert from the *Radio Times* of October 1943 for 'The Ancient Mariner' on the Schools Programme. With evacuation and shortages of books, schools' programmes became central to much teaching during the war.

There were also talks, on 'The House at Westminster', by Megan Lloyd George, MP, and in 'World Affairs' by the likes of Stephen King-Hall and Vernon Bartlett. Then there were regular concerts by BBC orchestras and broadcasts by children's choirs, and child performers.

Most popular, however, was drama, often in the form of serials. There were serial readings of *What Katy Did*, *Ivanhoe*, and *The Water Babies*, and serial drama productions of *Nicholas Nickleby*, *Little Women*, *Little Lord Fauntleroy* and *The Prisoner of Zenda*. One landmark was the production of several programmes of songs and 'Uncle Remus' stories by black American soldiers.

Every Wednesday five minutes of the programme was set aside for prayers, while on Sundays religious subjects were covered, such as Dorothy Sayers' series of religious plays, *The Man Born to be King*.

INTERNATIONAL

THE OVERSEAS SERVICE

In 1932 the BBC had started its Empire Service, broadcasting to English speakers across the Empire. The first foreign-language service, in Arabic, began as late as January 1938; programmes in German, French, and Italian followed later that year. In November 1939, after the addition of Spanish and Portuguese, the Empire Service was renamed the Overseas Service. By the end of 1940, it was broadcasting in 34 languages.

The prevalence of radio had transformed the importance of the speech. Only a few people would have heard, for instance, Lincoln's Gettysburg Address; now millions could

In October 1940 the 14-year-old Princess Elizabeth gave her first speech on 'Children's Hour', along with her 10-year-old sister Margaret Rose.

hear a speech on their wireless. Churchill was the perfect man for this; the King, however, was not, yet he was a most popular speaker; no audience in 1940 was larger than the 24 million who listened to his Empire Day speech. Every Christmas Day, he gave a speech to the people of the Empire; and men stood to attention as they listened at home. The Queen did her bit too: one memorable talk was delivered on 14 June 1940, the day Paris fell, in which she conveyed the sympathy and admiration of the women of Britain for their sisters in France.

On Sunday 13 October, Princess Elizabeth gave her first broadcast, to the children of the Empire on 'Children's Hour', including a special message to evacuated children, especially abroad. The speech was recorded and included that evening in the first of the weekly 15-minute programmes called 'Hello Children!' for evacuees in North America, Australia, New Zealand, and South Africa, which included messages from parents and talks or stories on topics of the moment. For North America there was also a half-hour programme every Sunday night, comprising historical plays, topical items, special programmes for younger children, news talks and regional items to remind children of home.

The broadcasting organisations of Canada, Australia, New Zealand, South Africa and the USA worked with the BBC to keep parents and children in touch through two-way message programmes, 'Children Calling Home', to North America once a month and to Australia and South Africa every eight weeks.

With large numbers of Imperial troops on the battlefronts, the

Evacuees boarding a boat to take them overseas in 1940. That October, special programmes began for the 'seavacuees', as they were called, on the Overseas Service.

TOGETHER

'Together' poster of Empire forces. With increasing numbers of Empire troops in Britain, the BBC broadcast programmes for them and about them and their countries.

Overseas Service broadcast magazine programmes, music recitals, feature programmes, and popular songs. Shows of greetings between the troops and their friends and families 'back home', were popular. Examples included, for South Africans and Rhodesians, 'Song time in the Laager', and for Australians and New Zealanders, 'Anzacs calling Home'. There were shows for members of the forces from the West Indies, while the Canadian Broadcasting Unit organised programmes from camps, clubs, and hospitals, including programmes in French for French-Canadians. In the autumn a programme in Maltese for Maltese subjects serving or working in Britain was introduced, as well as regular programmes recorded at the American Eagle Club, transmitted on the North American Service.

In the other direction there was, from 1940, 'Dominion Commentary' – a regular series of talks originating in Canada, Australia, New Zealand and South Africa, while Canada, Australia, New Zealand and India broadcast entertainment for their troops stationed in Great Britain.

The North American service was broadcast for seven and a half hours every night for listeners in the USA, Canada, Newfoundland, and the West Indies. There were specialised programmes for the West Indies (four times a week), Newfoundland (twice), and for Canada (twice a night).

In autumn 1942 the Variety Department produced 'Let's Get Acquainted', a series featuring top variety stars from both sides of the Atlantic, designed to promote understanding and friendship between Britain and America. In February 1944 came the first edition of the weekly programme 'Transatlantic

American reporter Quentin Reynolds with actress Diana Barrymore and a member of the RAF Eagle Squadron, made up of American volunteers. Reynolds made many moving broadcasts to his homeland.

In June 1940 General Charles de Gaulle broadcast on the BBC a call to his fellow Frenchmen for continued resistance; this resistance movement later became the Free French Forces.

Call – People to People', which was broadcast simultaneously in Britain and the United States.

Broadcasts for British forces overseas started in November 1942, with a service to the Middle East. On 10 January 1943, this became the Overseas Forces Programme, broadcasting to listeners in the Middle East for more than six hours a day; this had doubled by June, and was extended to cover from the Burmese frontier of India to the west coast of Africa. In November, it grew to twenty hours a day, covering the south Atlantic, Latin America, the United States and Canada. It also enlarged its scope, no longer broadcasting just for Britons fighting abroad; it now produced programmes for civilians in India, the West Indies, the United States and other countries. In June 1944 the

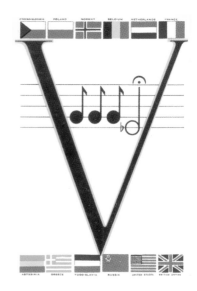

'V for Victory', and its musical notation. The 'V' became a symbol of resistance and hope across the nations fighting the Axis powers, some of whose flags are shown.

Poster displaying a shortened version of de Gaulle's speech. Leaflets were made of it and dropped by the RAF over occupied and Vichy France to encourage resistance.

programme for British Forces Overseas was reconstituted as the General Overseas Service.

On 17 June 1940 the French government asked the Germans for an armistice. The following day General de Gaulle spoke to the French people on the BBC from London, calling for continued resistance, and beginning the Free French Movement. From that day a daily five-minute slot was given to the Free French organisation, during which they broadcast '*Les Français parlent aux Français*'.

By late 1940 London had become the seat of governments-in-exile for Norway, Belgium, Holland, Poland, Czechoslovakia, Yugoslavia and Greece, as well as the headquarters of de Gaulle; each used the BBC to address their people at home. During 1940, King Haakon and the Crown Prince of Norway broadcast on a number of occasions; the Netherlands had a special slot entitled 'Radio Oranje', which began in July with a broadcast by Queen Wilhelmina. The Czechs also had a slot, as did the Belgians, who were given a special programme in French and Flemish on alternate days. In this slot on 14 January 1941, Victor de La Veleye, a Belgian policitian and broadcaster with free-Belgian radio, suggested using the letter 'V' (for victory) to symbolise resistance in Europe. Nothing happened at first, but by March evidence showed that use of the sign was spreading in Belgium, northern France and other occupied countries. On 6 June, 'Colonel Britton' (Douglas Ritchie) began a weekly broadcast, giving instructions to what he called the 'V' Army. At the end of June, the letter V in morse – three dots and a dash – became the signature tune of the series, in the form of the opening of Beethoven's Fifth Symphony.

Programme for the Royal Philharmonic Society's Summer Concert of June 1942, 'under the patronage of the Allied Governments' and broadcast live on the BBC.

Music was cleverly used by the French programme. Traditional tunes had new, anti-Nazi words set to them and were sung on the air. In occupied France, the tunes were then whistled; those in the know recognised the sentiment, yet to others, it was totally innocent.

FOREIGN RADIO STATIONS

In the first months of the war, with the dearth of news coming from the BBC, many began to turn to other stations in the search for information. One of these was the German station

A COMPLETE BIOGRAPHY OF
LORD
HAW-HAW
OF
ZEESEN
BY
JONAH BARRINGTON
AND
FENWICK

Lord Haw-Haw of Zeesen book cover, published in 1940, when Haw-Haw was seen as funny. Zeesen was one of the German stations broadcasting propaganda in English.

at Zeesen, one of several stations that broadcast an English-language 'news' programme. Here they encountered 'Lord Haw-Haw'. The name was coined by radio critic Jonah Barrington, who described the broadcaster as speaking 'English of the haw-haw, damn-it-get-out-of-my-way variety.' Although the name became synonymous with William Joyce, Barrington was actually referring to Norman Baillie-Stewart, a Nazi sympathiser and one of a number of announcers, including Joyce, who later took over the role.

In the unpredictable way of entertainment, Haw-Haw caught on. Like most radio stars, he had his own catchphrase, 'Germany calling, Germany calling', which he pronounced, 'Jairminy calling'. In Britain, as early as September 1939, there were fashionable 'wireless parties', where people would gather round a short-wave set to listen. The *Tatler* commented, 'You never failed to get some good laughs out of him, which was more than could be said about most of the BBC's comic turns'. Many did find him humorous, although others regarded him as omniscient, as when he was alleged to have stated that Darlington Town Hall clock was two minutes slow, which it was. The newspapers speculated on his identity, one suggestion being a former teacher at a Scottish school. Some suggested that it was unpatriotic to listen to him, while others thought the BBC should give the greatest publicity to the broadcasts, his claims, they said, being so ridiculous. By the autumn of

1940 the fad was over; the fall of France and the beginning of the Blitz meant that few still saw the war in the same humorous light.

Another source of German propaganda was Radio Luxembourg. The BBC was the only broadcasting organisation licensed in the UK, but commercial stations in Europe could be picked up in Britain, such as the English language service of Radio Luxembourg, begun in 1933. At the end of September 1939 the Luxembourg government closed the station down to protect the country's neutrality, but after the German invasion in 1940, the station was taken over and used for English-language propaganda broadcasts.

Some people wanted the BBC to produce its own propaganda in opposition to that of the Germans, and in particular, Haw-Haw. The BBC countered that its reputation for truth was far too valuable to lose in an attempt to outdo Goebbels at his own game. They took a different line: from late 1939 W.A. Sinclair broadcast a weekly analysis of German propaganda in 'The Voice of the Nazi'.

In 1940, this line was extended to the overseas service. The daily 'Listening Post' on the Pacific, Eastern, African, and North American Services looked at aspects of Nazi propaganda, showing how Goebbels told one story in German and different stories in other languages. A year later, similar

William Joyce is the name most usually associated with Lord Haw-Haw, although there were several announcers given the name, including ex-British Army officer, Norman Baillie-Stewart.

THE WORST CAUSE IN THE WORLD
(WITH THE BEST PROPAGANDA)

THE BEST CAUSE IN THE WORLD
(WITH THE WORST PROPAGANDA)

David Low cartoon from October 1939, contrasting the German attitude to propaganda, in the form of Goebbels, with the British response, in the form of Low's creation, Colonel Blimp.

broadcasts in the North American and Pacific Services entitled 'Flashback' contrasted what Germany and Italy were saying with what they had said a year before.

As well as eight news bulletins a day, the Germans received a regular feature, called '*Vormarsch der Freiheit*' (March of Freedom), and special programmes, including drama, monologues, dialogues and music, aimed at specific sections of the population: workers, soldiers, airmen, sailors, peasants, housewives and intellectuals. These programmes included 'Frau Wernicke', 'Kurt and Willi' and 'Lance-Corporal Hirnschal'. In 1943, a separate service for Austria was launched, which by the end of the year included five bulletins a day.

It is an interesting fact that in the last weeks of the war, when they were cut off from contact with their high command, many German commanders used the BBC German Service for news of what was happening.

FOR YOUR INFORMATION

WITH THE DEARTH of news in the winter of 1939 came calls to cut news bulletins to the pre-war two a day, but in the summer of 1940, the *Blitzkrieg* revived interest. By that time the bulletins had been trimmed to 7am and 8am (on Sundays 9am), and in the afternoon at 1pm, 6pm, 9pm, and midnight. There was also a daily bulletin in Welsh and two weekly bulletins in Gaelic; these continued throughout the war. The period after the 6pm bulletin was devoted to official announcements.

One problem was the need to give the news while ensuring that no details were given which could help the enemy. Thus locations were rarely specific: 'somewhere in the home counties', etc. The military authorities wanted to keep a very tight rein on the news, but this did not go down well with the public. Mass Observation reports contained the likes of, 'if present policy of withholding air-raid details continues, all news will be distrusted', and the contrast between announcers 'stating casualties were slight and no material damage done, and information received by post from residents'.

Advertisement for the radio programme 'Kitchen Front' in 'Food Facts', hints published by the Ministry of Food in newspapers and magazines, this one from December 1940.

Always turn on your wireless at 8.15 every morning to hear the useful hints and recipes.

Frederick ('Freddy') Grisewood, one of the BBC's regular announcers/ newsreaders. In 1940 announcers became household names when, for security reasons, they began to give their names on air.

The government became worried about the Germans broadcasting fake news (they used the term then!) or instructions. Up to this point newsreaders had been anonymous, but in the summer of 1940, with the fall of France and the subsequent invasion scare, the BBC decided to use a small group of announcers and newsreaders who would identify themselves thus: 'Here is the news and this is Alvar Liddell reading it'. Listeners would become familiar with their voices and spot imitations, although some took exception to what they considered self-advertisement. There still remained concerns that the 'BBC accent' could easily be imitated; it was thought a regional accent was

Detail from a wartime Jacqmar 'propaganda' scarf, named, 'Here is the News, and this is Jacqmar presenting it', the phrase by which BBC newsreaders identified themselves.

harder to imitate, and in November 1941, Yorkshireman Wilfred Pickles was brought in. It is difficult now to understand the controversy this provoked in some quarters, particularly his farewell catchphrase '... and to all in the North, good neet'.

News bulletins consisted of communiqués and reports, not only from London but also from the regions. Bulletins increasingly contained first-hand accounts of the experiences of those in the news or on-the-spot impressions from BBC war correspondents. The news was often followed by news talks and 'postscripts', which sought to give context to it.

In 1941, Yorkshireman Wilfred Pickles was added to the list of BBC announcers in an attempt to bring in regional accents, which would be more difficult for Germans to imitate.

From March 1940 Maurice Healy gave twelve talks after the 9 o'clock news on Sunday evenings; these would become the Sunday Postscripts. He was succeeded by J.B. Priestley, whose homespun style, delivered in his Bradford accent, was very popular, although not among some Conservative MPs who considered him left-wing, even unpatriotic, for remarks like 'woolly, pussy-footed officialdom', and his insistence that post-war the country must not go back to the poverty of the thirties. He finished in October 1940, after which the Postscripts were given by a number of speakers, including Eleanor Roosevelt in November 1942.

Sometimes the BBC itself was not just an observer. On 8 December 1940 a land mine fell in Portland Place; Broadcasting House caught fire, one studio being burnt out. One week later a delayed-action bomb smashed through a seventh-floor window, finishing up in the music library two floors below. It exploded just after 9pm, killing seven BBC staff. Listeners heard the explosion, but Bruce Belfrage,

Postscripts

J. B. PRIESTLEY

Cover of *Postscripts*, by J.B. Priestley. At the time of Dunkirk, Priestly began broadcasting his weekly Postscripts, which proved controversial, being loved by many and hated by a vociferous minority.

reading the news, paused briefly, then calmly continued.

Before the war, outdoor broadcasts were mainly from sporting and public events. Now they came into their own. One memorable early wartime broadcast featured Charles Gardner on the cliffs of south-east England during the Battle of Britain giving an excited account of a dogfight over the Channel. There were broadcasts from factory benches and canteens, and of Civil Defence demonstrations. Sporting programmes, however, were not forgotten, and many of the principal events were covered.

In 1938 the News Department had developed a mobile unit that could travel to any part of the country, record a story, and get it back to a studio. The apparatus was compact enough to fit into a car, light enough to be carried, yet robust enough to withstand the rigours of transport. With this, the BBC was able to record air raids from roof-tops, from fireboats on the Thames, tanks going into the attack, or the roar of aircraft taking off.

On D-Day the BBC's War Reporting Unit came into operation using a newly developed 'mighty midget' disc recorder which weighed just 42lb and could be operated without the assistance of engineers. Using this, many broadcasts of action were obtained in the weeks following D-Day when BBC war correspondents landed with the troops on the beaches, and jumped with airborne troops.

Since 1934, Cecil Middleton had broadcast a popular weekly gardening programme, 'In Your Garden'. 'Mr Middleton', as he was known, had a unique style for the time:

As the war progressed, the BBC went to Europe with the invasion forces, delivering outside broadcasts called 'War Report'. Here, Pierre LeFevre broadcasts from Normandy.

informal, humorous and chatty, speaking to the listener as if to a friend. Off the air during the first days of the war, he was back on Sunday 17 September. The Ministry of Agriculture sought and received the BBC's and Middleton's help in the 'Dig for Victory' campaign. 'In Your Garden' was broadcast on Sunday afternoons throughout the war.

In July 1940 John Morgan introduced the series 'Backs to the Land', a weekly five-minute programme for smallholders, which ran for the rest of the war. Early in 1942 the BBC began a series for allotment holders: 'Radio Allotment', broadcast from a real allotment in a square near Broadcasting House. The broadcasts began from scratch, with the BBC news

Middleton's Garden Guide was published in 1945. Cecil Middleton was the first radio gardener, a great favourite throughout the war.

122 WARTIME RECIPES
broadcast by Frederick Grisewood,
Mabel Constanduros and others, specially selected by the Ministry of Food.

The Kitchen Front, a recipe book, with a cover by Fougasse (Cyril Kenneth Bird). 'Kitchen Front' was broadcast daily, giving advice, tips and recipes from 1940 to 1945.

team, Wynford Vaughan-Thomas, Raymond Glendenning, Stewart MacPherson, and Michael Standing preparing the ground, sowing, etc. Their lack of knowledge was designed to encourage novices to take on allotments.

On 4 December 1939, with the nation's fitness in mind, a religious 'Thought for To-day' was broadcast under the title 'Lift up your hearts', followed by ten minutes of physical exercises for men and women, on alternate mornings. In September 1943, the 'Daily dozen' programmes began, with separate sets of exercises for men and women each morning.

With January 1940 came food rationing and, at 10.45am, 'The Kitchen in Wartime', which continued until July 1941. For a fortnight during April 1940, a nightly five-minute series on behalf of the Ministry of Food entitled 'Feed the Brute' was broadcast after the 6pm news. It starred the popular comediennes, Ethel and Doris Waters, in their characters, Gert and Daisy. Their sketches were a comic treatment of domestic cooking problems, including useful recipes. Well over half of working-class housewives listened to these talks, even though the broadcast time was unsuitable for many housewives.

Subsequently, on 25 June the five-minute long 'Kitchen Front' programme was introduced – 'a talk about what to eat and where to get it' – and this continued throughout the war. Note had been taken of the timing, the show being broadcast each morning after the 8 o'clock news.

Gert and Daisy, alias comediennes Elsie and Doris Waters (Jack Warner's sisters), who regularly appeared on 'Kitchen Front' and other BBC programmes, seen here giving a cookery demonstration.

Presenters varied and with them the format. 'Gert and Daisy' returned in late 1941, and there were other comedy formats, including the 'Buggins family'. Some were more serious, such as the 'Radio Doctor' (Charles Hill) who appeared from May 1942, giving talks on healthy diets and health generally. From October 1943 the Monday edition of the 'Kitchen Front' was replaced by the 'Fuel Front', while the Saturday edition became 'Make-do and Mend'. Other women's programmes included 'Calling All Women', and 'Woman's Page'.

The Minister of Fuel and Power broadcast on the Fuel Economy Campaign in the Sunday Postscript in June 1942. The following day, fuel-saving hints began to appear in the 'Kitchen Front'; soon afterwards 'Fuel Flashes', by Freddie Grisewood, were introduced after the 6pm news on alternate days. On one occasion he brought in his daughter, Sergeant Anne Grisewood, to speak on fuel economy in the WAAF.

In its war plan the BBC was to cease schools broadcasts for the first two weeks of war to facilitate evacuation, after which

Girls working at home following the schools programme. With evacuation some schools in inner cities were closed, leaving remaining children without education; for some children, schools broadcasts were their only education.

it would continue the broadcasts as long as circumstances permitted. In the event six special broadcasts a day began as early as 5 September 1939, in an attempt to interest and amuse evacuated schoolchildren. Schools broadcasts became especially important; many evacuated schools were unable to obtain textbooks, and the programmes formed the basis of their syllabus. In places where schools were not allowed to open, teachers visited small groups of children in private houses, and used the broadcasts with them.

Before the war, pamphlets had been issued to illustrate the broadcasts, but these had to be abandoned because of paper restrictions. To overcome this, more and more use was made of dramatisation and narrative using the BBC Schools Repertory Company.

In 1942, to educate and raise morale among British service personnel, the Army instituted ABCA (Army Bureau of Current Affairs) discussion groups, while on the home front civil defence organisations, in particular the fire service, began their own groups. To augment this the BBC produced programmes designed for group listening; by late in the year over a thousand such groups listened weekly to programmes such as 'Westminster and Beyond', and 'Man's Place in Nature'. By 1943 these were joined by youth discussion groups, which had their own programme: 'To Start You Talking'.

Cabinet ministers and other government speakers broadcast frequently, speaking of their plans and reporting on their progress. In 1941 there were, on the home and overseas programmes, 225 such broadcasts, 44 by members of the War Cabinet. However,

a Mass Observation report noted: 'there are numerous indications that the ministerial appeal and pep talk has been losing its impact, owing to too many talks of the same kind, often by Ministers who are not expert broadcasters.'

By 1942 about 10 per cent of broadcasting time on the home and forces programmes was given to talks, including talks by Ministers, war despatches and commentaries, Sunday Postscripts, discussions, and literary, scientific and religious talks. There were also documentaries, most of which were on aspects of the war; many looked at the regions of the United Kingdom, and their particular role in the struggle – mining, farming, fishing, shipbuilding, industry, and so on.

Minister of Food Lord Woolton, broadcasting on the BBC. Many ministers took to the air, but unlike Churchill, few had the ability or the training to do it successfully.

THE FORCES PROGRAMME

From the start of the war, with its broadcasting confined to a single service, the BBC began to plan a second channel, whose primary aim was to entertain the troops in France, while in addition supplementing the Home Service. The boring, bitterly cold winter of the 'phoney war' in France made it all the more pressing. Meetings were held with representatives of the War Office, Admiralty, and Air Ministry, all of which supported the idea. BBC staff went to France to find out what the BEF liked to hear and how, when and where they could listen. The BBC explained that it wanted to give the troops the entertainment they wanted, not what others thought was good for them to hear.

In February 1940, the new programme came into being. There was some debate over a name for the new service: the Services Programme, the Forces Programme, or the BEF Programme. The choice fell on the Forces Programme. Listening was usually a communal activity in the services, in canteens and so on, so light music, dance music, cinema organ, and variety of every kind made up the bulk of what was provided, although as with home listeners the news was most popular.

Popular early shows included 'Sandy's Half-Hour' with the Canadian Sandy MacPherson on the BBC theatre organ, and 'Have You Met Annette?' featuring Betty Astell as radio sweetheart to servicemen. Camp concerts were broadcast from barracks, aerodromes, and naval stations, as well as the 'Ack-Ack,

OPPOSITE: There was an urgent need for a second channel aimed at the services. By February 1940 all the necessary work had been completed and the Forces Programme began broadcasting.

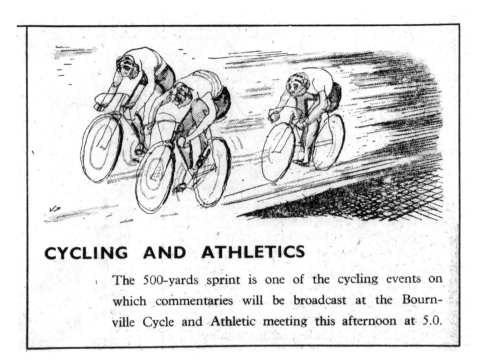

CYCLING AND ATHLETICS

The 500-yards sprint is one of the cycling events on which commentaries will be broadcast at the Bournville Cycle and Athletic meeting this afternoon at 5.0.

Cycling and athletics programme from the *Radio Times*, May 1940. Sporting programmes were popular among the services, and a wide range of sports features was broadcast on the Forces Programme.

Beer-Beer' shows dedicated to personnel serving in isolated anti-aircraft, barrage-balloon, and searchlight units. Soon, with early reveille in mind, broadcasting to the forces began at 6.30am.

This diet of music, variety and news also proved popular among civilian listeners; some liked to think that they were sharing the experience with their friends and relatives in the forces. By 1942 civilians made up 90 per cent of listeners and more attention was given to the civilian home front.

With the end of the phoney war and the fall of France, Forces broadcasting became less light-hearted; by the autumn of 1940 the Forces Programme contained more spoken material and a regular if small amount of serious music. These were joined by programmes for industry, including 'Music While You Work' and 'Workers' Playtime'. Another cause of change was the increasing number of empire troops in the country. Newsletters and other programmes made especially

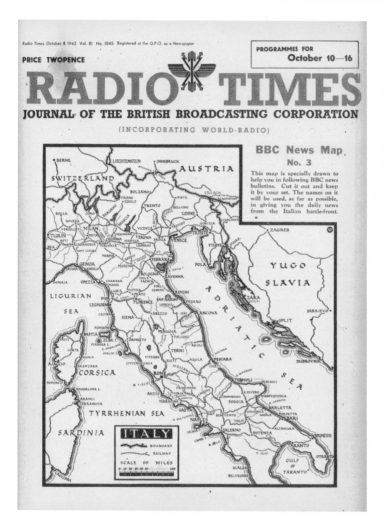

Radio Times,
October 1943.
This map, for the
Italian campaign,
and similar ones
covering other
combat areas,
were produced
as an aid to
following the war
news bulletins.

for the troops from Canada, Australia, New Zealand, and India were regularly given.

On Christmas Eve, 1940, the BBC introduced a weekly programme for troops in India, soon followed by others for the RAF in the East and those training in Canada, to the Mediterranean Fleet, Iceland, Tobruk, Malta, Gibraltar, Palestine, and many other places. As the number of troops in the Middle East and India increased, such occasional programmes

NAVY MIXTURE
Joyce Grenfell (left) and Adèle Dixon (right) star with Charles Harrison, ·Carroll Gibbons, and Will Fyffe at 5.15 p.m.

Forces programmes were not only for the Army; there were programmes for the other services, the RAF, the Merchant Navy, and the Royal Navy, such as 'Navy Mixture', from 1943.

proved insufficient, and daily schedules were introduced. Christened the 'General Overseas Service', it expanded from its small beginnings until it was broadcasting for twenty-two hours a day right across the globe. While planned for serving men on all the fronts, for civilian listeners abroad it constituted an alternative to the other BBC Overseas Services, but it could not be heard in Britain without special equipment.

In 1941 'Women at War' began, for women in the services, as did 'Irish Half-Hour', designed for Irish members of the forces, while for the Merchant Navy there was 'The Blue Peter' (no relation to the children's programme), recordings of which were transmitted all round the world, and 'Under the Red Duster' (the nickname of the Merchant Navy flag). To foster closer ties between the services came 'Tom, Dick, and Harry', about the off-duty adventures of a soldier, sailor, and an airman. The 'BBC Dancing Club' came into existence with Victor Silvester as instructor, while for swing fans there was the 'Radio Rhythm Club',

A Manual designed for the guidance of all officers in the conduct of talks and discussions on Current Affairs. With Preface by the Secretary of State for War.
NEW REVISED EDITION...JULY, 1943

THE ABCA HANDBOOK

ISSUED BY THE ARMY BUREAU OF CURRENT AFFAIRS
CROWN COPYRIGHT RESERVED

ABCA handbook, 1943. ABCA was set up in 1941 to increase morale among the troops by discussing current affairs. To support it the BBC broadcast programmes designed for group listening.

featuring Harry Parry. Music was particularly popular, and appropriate for the particular listening needs of the

here is your own show—

'Women at War', a magazine for women in the three services, begins in the Forces programme on Monday. Here's all about it, by Robert MacDermot.

forces, and that year there were, on average, over twenty music shows a week by popular dance bands.

One special consideration for the programme planners was that, if the broadcast programme did not please the listening troops, they could always turn the dial to find something more appealing on a foreign station, and often that meant an enemy station. The Germans responded by broadcasting a forces programme for British listeners. This mainly consisted of light music and jazz, with an occasional (propagandised) news bulletin. In the summer of 1942 troops in Egypt were regularly listening to a German programme on which they heard the song 'Lilli Marlene', by singer Lale Andersen, which soon became their favourite whistling and marching tune.

In early 1942 Andersen recorded the song in English, translated by Norman Baillie-Stewart, a former British Army officer working for the Germans. In 1944, Tommie Connor wrote new English lyrics; this version was recorded by Anne Shelton and also became a huge hit.

However, this all showed how easy it was for the German radio to insinuate itself and its

In 1941, the weekly 'Women at War' was introduced, 'a magazine programme for and by women in war jobs': the services, factory workers, nurses, land girls, and civil defence workers.

'Lilli Marlene' sheet music from 1944. The original German song was adopted by the British 8th Army, and English words put to it, during the North Africa campaign.

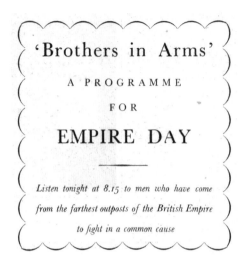

'Brothers in Arms'

A PROGRAMME

FOR

EMPIRE DAY

Listen tonight at 8.15 to men who have come

from the farthest outposts of the British Empire

to fight in a common cause

A special Empire Day programme, May 1940. Soon France would fall, and Britain would stand alone – that is, if you forgot the empire. Programmes like this helped people remember.

propaganda into the Allied forces, and the BBC more than ever realised that it needed to hold the troops' attention by giving them the sort of entertainment they wanted. This in turn brought criticism from those who believed that the forces were being fed a diet of 'jazz', and 'sickly and maudlin programmes', which undermined their ferocity while what they needed was stirring martial music.

It is interesting to note that 'Lilli Marlene' fell prey to such criticism not only in Britain, but also in Germany where Joseph Goebbels, the Minister of Propaganda banned the song for not being military enough. However, by a trick of fate, the German station was bombed and most of its records destroyed; that night, in desperation the station was forced to play whatever they could find, including 'Lilli Marlene'. The Men of the Afrika Korps loved it, Field Marshal Rommel asked the station to play the song every night, and Goebbels was forced to change his mind.

In Britain, the BBC on the other hand was giving way to pressure from the puritans. Following a review of programmes in conjunction with the War Office, changes were made. Stirring programmes like 'Marching On' and 'Into Battle' and more serious music were introduced. Yet this did not silence the critics; as late as March 1944 Earl Winterton said in Parliament:

I listen from an English broadcasting point of view to the half-hour musical programme which Germany sends out principally for its troops. I must confess it seems to me infinitely better than ours – patriotic songs, light opera, an occasional modern song, and even when the Germans attempt the form of crooning I think it is less objectionable than the Cockney attempt to imitate the worst type of American accent.

Vera Lynn was another target of criticism; in 1939 her recording of 'We'll Meet Again', had led to her being named 'the Forces' sweetheart' by the *Daily Express* after she came top in a poll of British servicemen. She began to appear in BBC shows, including 'Starlight', a fifteen-minute show for troops overseas. This was followed by her best-known wartime series, 'Sincerely Yours – Vera Lynn' in November 1941. Taking the popular form of a letter to the men of the forces, the series was a hit, attracting over 20 per cent of the population. But it too became a target for criticism. In response, the BBC decided to rest 'Sincerely Yours', and in July 1942 it announced a 'crooner ban'. A 'Dance Music Policy Committee' censored songs, male crooners, and 'insincere and over-sentimental' female singers, banning over thirty singers.

'Sincerely Yours', starring Vera Lynn: 'To the men of the Forces: a letter in words and music.' As well as music, there were messages to husbands, and to new fathers.

In 1942, a trickle of American troops, soon to become a flood, began arriving in Britain. As with the Canadian troops, the BBC offered to provide special services and American entertainment for them, and this was gratefully accepted. At first this took the form of a short sports bulletin every night. With the help of the BBC they soon created their own broadcasting system, the 'American Forces Network', which opened on Independence Day 1943. It was made up of several low-power transmitters sited wherever there

The Radio Times of the British Forces Station operating in Northern Italy, 21 April 1945   Vol. I No. 4

RADIO TIMES

APRIL 22
TO
APRIL 28

OF THE BRITISH FORCES STATION OPERATING IN NORTHERN ITALY
234 METRES, 1285 KCS.

Judith Anderson,
who was born in South Australia was lured by
the lights of Broadway, and after many strug-
gling and hungry months got her first real part
in "Dear Brutus". After David Belasco had
seen her, she wasassigned up for "The Dove".
Recently she has been lauded with many adj-
ectives for her work in "Family Portrait", and
her part in the film "Rebecca".
    She first appeared in Shakespeare as the
Queen in Hamlet, with John Gielgud and
gave her London performance of Lady Macbeth in 1937.

Maurice Evans,
is a naturalized American, born in England.
A year before coming to America, Evans
gave a four hour performance of Hamlet at
the Old Vic, and attained International ac-
claim. His American debut was as Romeo to
Katharine Cornell's Juliet. The brilliant success
of this led to interpretations of Richard II,
Henry IV, Hamlet and Twelfth Night and
Macbeth.

"... all the perfumes of Arabia
will not sweeten this little hand"
(ACT V, SCENE I)

WILLIAM SHAKESPEARE'S
MACBETH
WITH MAURICE EVANS & JUDITH ANDERSON

will be broadcast on Shakespeare's birthday,
Monday, 23 April at 9.30 pm.

MAKE A NOTE OF THESE PROGRAMMES

SUNDAY	11.02 -	Bournemouth Central Gardens Bandstand.
MONDAY	19.00 -	Quiz : 20 00-St. George and the Dragon : 21.30-Macbeth.
TUESDAY	21.30 -	From the Rainbow Room, New York.
WEDNESDAY	21.45 -	Services Music Hall.
THURSDAY	19.00 -	From the pages of an old Radio Times.
FRIDAY	21.30 -	Your Hit Parade.
SATURDAY	17.45 -	A letter from Home.

Radio Times for the forces in Italy, April 1945. Special editions of the Radio Times were issued for the forces overseas, listing the programmes available locally.

were large concentrations of American troops. The programmes consisted partly of shows from the Forces Programme but mainly of recordings of American radio shows, made in the States and sent over to Britain.

The 'girlfriends of the forces' shows continued to be well received, and in 1942 Doreen Villiers began broadcasting to the 8th Army in 'A Date for the Desert', while Kay Cavendish and Sandy MacPherson began a series for troops in India. A special weekly programme for overseas, 'Tommy Handley's Half-Hour', appeared throughout the year, on one occasion featuring Hollywood star Edward G. Robinson as its special guest.

New programmes in 1943 included 'Variety Bandbox' and 'China Flight', for the RAF serving in China and 'Out of the Blue' for RAF personnel elsewhere. The Radio Padre, the Reverend Ronald Selby Wright, spoke each week.

On 21 January 1944 the BBC announced that, starting on 27 February, the Forces Programme would be dropped, and the General Overseas Service would become the second programme throughout the United Kingdom, becoming 'The General Forces Programme', and keeping most of the popular features of the old one.

General Eisenhower, Supreme Commander of the Allied Expeditionary Force, wanted all the American, British, and Canadian forces under his command to share a single radio programme. The idea took shape, becoming the Allied Expeditionary Forces Programme, which went on the air at

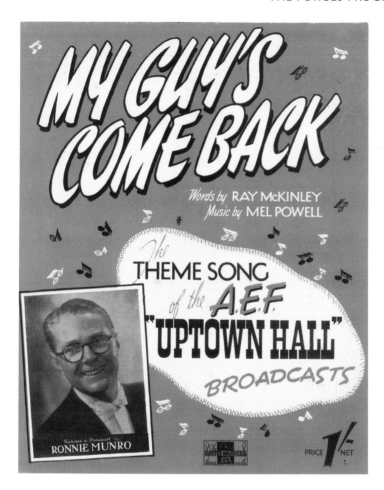

'My Guy's Come Back' sheet music, from 1945. The Allied Expeditionary Forces Programme began broadcasting to the United Nations invasion forces on 7 June 1944 – the day after D-Day.

5.55am on 7 June 1944 – D-Day plus 1. The AEFP, as it was known, broadcast for seventeen hours daily, beginning and ending each day's broadcasting with prayers. The BBC was responsible for the direction of the AEFP and its transmission from the United Kingdom, with the full co-operation of the American and Canadian Services radios. The programme was made up of shows from all three countries, including Major Glenn Miller's American Band of the AEF and other programmes specially produced for the AEF, such as 'Combat Diary' – daily war reports from both service and civilian correspondents.

THE END OF THE WAR

B Y THE SPRING of 1945 German resistance was crumbling. News bulletins brought reports of Allied advances on all fronts, and late on 2 May 1945, the BBC interrupted its programme to tell its listeners that German radio had announced the death of Hitler. Two days later the German armies in the west surrendered to Field Marshall Montgomery; people expected the end of the war to be announced, but nothing happened.

The problem was that Britain, the USA, and the Soviet Union had agreed to announce the end of the war together, and German forces were still fighting in the east. That weekend, speculation was rife; on Monday 7 May, the *Evening Standard* led with the headline: 'This may be VE-Night: any hour now.' Hundreds of thousands began to congregate in city centres, believing the end of hostilities would be announced at any moment.

For the BBC this caused many headaches; that day a thousand troops had been brought together and kept waiting for three hours in readiness for the official declaration, which finally came at 8pm. VE-Day would not be that night, but the following day, which would be the first of a two-day bank holiday. The timing had to allow all three leaders to announce peace simultaneously to their countries, so Churchill would make the official announcement at 3pm. The troops were sent back, to be brought together again the following day.

OPPOSITE:
VE-Day outdoor broadcast: Howard Marshall, the BBC's Director of War reporting outside Buckingham Palace. The BBC broadcast the Declaration of War in 1939; now it would report the peace celebrations.

German troops surrendering to US forces in the spring of 1945. As German resistance in the west crumbled, listeners at home eagerly awaited the announcement of the end of the war.

Victory hat. The V campaign, which started slowly in 1940, had caught on and spread like wildfire. The 'V' played a prominent part in the victory decorations.

As with the outbreak of war, the BBC's programme for the day was hastily reshuffled. Up to 3pm they remained unchanged, including 'the Daily Dozen' and 'Kitchen Front', and – strangely for a bank holiday – the schools' programme and 'Workers Playtime'. Then at 3pm Churchill would address the nation, followed by 'Victory Celebrations'. Later, at 8pm, there was a service of thanksgiving, and at 9pm, the King. His speech, and Churchill's, were broadcast on the Home, Forces, and AEF programmes. For the crowds in town centres up and down the country, loudspeakers were often set up, so they could listen to the historic announcements.

Programmes that evening reflected the expected festivities, being mostly music. Instead of the usual

Crowds outside Parliament on VE-Day. Big Ben shows 3pm; when Churchill would announce the end of the war in Europe, his speech relayed to the crowds over loudspeakers.

midnight shutdown, the Home Service went on until 2am, although the Forces Programme went off, as usual, after the 11 o'clock news.

On 9 May, the second of the two VE-Days, the wireless diet was similar: music (appropriately including Sandy MacPherson, who had played in the first few days of the war), news, and religious services. The evening's broadcasts were again extended, this time to 1.30am.

King George VI addressing the nation; he hated broadcasting, but over the course of the war his had become a familiar voice and now he would speak on VE- and VJ-Day.

For the rest of the week there was a blend of normal programmes and victory related ones; on 10 May there was 'V-ITMA' and 'Victory sing-song', while that weekend, on 13 May the first performance was broadcast of Vaughan Williams' 'Thanksgiving for Victory', specially commissioned by the BBC.

With victory in Europe, the Allied armies set up their separate occupation zones. The need for an integrated service ceased, and the American Broadcasting Station in Europe, for which the BBC had provided transmitting stations and other facilities, shut down on 4 July. On 28 July the BBC's wartime broadcasting plan was brought to a close; the Allied Expeditionary Forces Programme closed down, and the home broadcasting service returned to its peacetime system of regional services, plus the Home Service and a new Light Programme. The introduction of the new programme went some way to calming the heated debate that had gone on throughout the war: should the BBC put out popular programmes such as 'ITMA', dance bands, crooners and comics, or should it try to educate the masses with classical music, educational debates, arts programmes and the like. With just one channel they had to try a balancing act, which as usual pleased nobody; now they could try both, with the Home Service going up market, and the Light Programme, as its name suggested, containing more popular light entertainment.

On 14 August the news of the Japanese surrender was given in a midnight broadcast by the new Prime Minister, Clement Attlee. Again, the following two days were designated public holidays, and again the BBC had an anxious time, preparing for a celebration with the date unknown. For three days preceding the Prime Minister's announcement the eighty-strong Luton Choral Society had been bussed to Bedford for a broadcast, which, in the event, never happened. Due to the late hour of the announcement, and the several stations involved, it was almost impossible to do much more than add in the King's speech, a religious service of thanksgiving and extended news bulletins. Once again, on the day itself the King addressed the nation and the Empire in a broadcast from his study at Buckingham Palace at 9pm.

With the end of conflict, programmes spawned by the war also finished; the 'Kitchen Front' and the 'Daily Dozen' both came to an end that September. Some programmes continued, of course: 'ITMA' would remain a favourite until Tommy Handley's death in January 1949, the 'Brains Trust' would go on answering obscure questions until May that year, and 'Much Binding in the Marsh', started in January 1944, continued until September 1950.

CONCLUSION

O VER SIX YEARS of war the young BBC of pre-war days had grown up. In 1929 the corporation had begun as an English-language-only broadcaster, with the mission 'to educate, inform and entertain' the nation. From the very beginning the BBC faced the impossible task of trying to please everyone. Being financed by the licence revenues, the government felt it should have control over the broadcaster, whereas the corporation saw itself as being non-partisan, and therefore independent.

Others saw its main task as education, especially cultural, so that the entertainment side would be of a more uplifting nature. Yet again, others saw this as elitist and patronising.

Information was in two forms, the news and talks. Before the war the BBC had produced only two news bulletins a day, both in the evening, at 6pm and 9pm. The government had agreed to limit the Corporation's news output after protests from the daily newspapers that earlier radio news bulletins would eat into their customer base.

Throughout the 1930s the BBC tried hard to solve these impossible problems, steering a middle course. The advent of war changed all that: with the amalgamation of all home channels into a single service the balancing problem became acute. The BBC responded with in-depth listener surveys, and populist entertainment interspersed with more serious programmes. It also found that serious topics could be looked at in a popular way; dull ministry information programmes

OPPOSITE: *BBC Calling All Nations* booklet, published in December 1942. The BBC broadcast solely in English before 1938, but by the end of the war it was broadcasting in forty-five languages worldwide.

William and the Brains Trust was published in April 1945. It is a sign of the programme's popularity that even William Brown would have an adventure around it.

were spiced up, as with the 'Kitchen Front', inspired by Gert and Daisy's popular 'Feed the Brute' programmes, and the 'Brains Trust'.

The wireless was the perfect medium for the communication of news, information and instructions from the government to the populace, and news bulletins suddenly became hourly, soon settling on six a day, at 7 and 8am (9am on Sundays), 1, 6, 9pm, and midnight, and there it would effectively remain after the war.

The government and the service high commands wanted to keep a tight rein on the information reaching the public; national security required that no information be given out that could be helpful to the enemy, but at the same time the BBC wished to ensure that the news which was given out was accurate, and fast. In terms of accuracy, the news given to the BBC was censored by the government, then

'Much Binding in the Marsh' sheet music, showing its three stars: Dicky Murdoch (previously of 'Band Waggon'), Kenneth Horne, and the orchestra leader, Sidney Torch. The show was broadcast from January 1944.

re-censored by BBC, so that no obviously false news would be broadcast. The need to counter German propaganda was soon recognised, but the corporation's view was that this should be done, not by producing British propaganda, but by presenting the truth, and rebutting enemy lies.

Pre-war, this policy had resulted in the BBC gaining a reputation for truthfulness; their insistence on keeping to the policy helped them retain this reputation. A Mass Observation report of 1941 stated: 'The radio is at present the most trusted of British sources of information.'

This reputation for truthfulness would pay dividends; in 1939 the BBC had been primarily a British affair, only broadcasting in languages other than English from 1938. By 1945, however, the Overseas and Empire Services covered most of the globe; this would continue, with the number of languages broadcast expanding and reception improving. On 1 May 1965 the service became the BBC World Service.

Before the war, BBC engineering operators were entirely men. By 1942 over five hundred women operators were working at transmitting stations and studios up and down the country.

Several wartime favourites continued in popularity post-war. ITMA postcards like this continued to be sold and used well after the war was over, as did the catchphrases.

AN ITMA WISECRACK — *Illustrated by Bert Thomas*

SILENCE

" It's that man again ! "

FURTHER READING

BOOKS

Brown, Mike, and Carol Harris. *Air Raids & Ration Books* (Sabrestorm, 2010) – Life on the Home Front.

Hanson, Neil. *Priestley's Wars* (Great Northern Books, 2008) – Includes section on 'Postscripts'.

Hill, Jonathan. *Old Radio Sets* (Shire, 1993) – Vintage radio sets.

Lynn, Vera. *Some Sunny Day* (Harper Collins, 2009) – Lynn's autobiography.

Murphy, Kate. *Behind the Wireless* (Palgrave Macmillan, 2016) – Women at the BBC.

WEBSITES

www.archive.org/details/OldTimeRadio-1940s – Downloads of original shows, including Robb Wilton, Arthur Askey and many more.

www.bbc.co.uk/archive – Old clips and information about past shows.

genome.ch.bbc.co.uk – Search old *Radio Times* entries (dates, programmes, etc.)

www.1940.co.uk – The 1940s Society. Their online magazine often includes articles about entertainment in the Second World War.

www.turnipnet.com – This focuses more on the 1950s than the '40s, but is well worth a look.

www.bl.uk/collection-guides/radio-broadcasts – British Library's sound archives.

bufvc.ac.uk/archives – British universities' sound archives.

www.radiomuseum.org – Many photographs of vintage radios.

graciefields.org – Information about one of the era's great stars.

www.jbpriestleysociety.com – Information about the author, Postscripts, etc.

www.facebook.com/groups/57058203383/ – The Dame Vera Lynn Appreciation Society.

www.bbc.co.uk/liverpool/localhistory/journey/stars/tommy_handley/itma.shtml – Includes information about Tommy Handley, 'ITMA', scripts, catchphrases, etc.

www.amazon.co.uk – The music section carries recordings of most radio stars of the period, while the book section carries many out-of-print second-hand books from the period, BBC handbooks, etc.

PLACES TO VISIT

If you've enjoyed this book you may wish to learn more.

The British Vintage Wireless and Television Museum, West Dulwich, London. Telephone: 020 8670 3667. Open by appointment only; please phone in advance.

Imperial War Museum, London, Lambeth Road, London SE1 6HZ. Website: www.iwm.org.uk

Imperial War Museum North, Trafford Wharf Road, Manchester M17 1TZ. Website: www.iwm.org.uk

Museum of Communication, 131 High Street, Burntisland, Scotland KY3 9AA. Telephone: 01592 874836. Email: enquiries@mocft.co.uk

The National Radio Centre, Bletchley Park, Sherwood Drive, Bletchley, Milton Keynes MK3 6EB. Telephone: 01908 640404. Email: info@bletchleypark.org.uk

The National Science and Media Museum, Little Horton Lane, Bradford BD1 1NQ. Telephone: 0844 856 3797. Website: www.scienceandmediamuseum.org.uk

Washford Radio Museum, Tropiquaria, Washford Cross, Watchet, Somerset TA23 0QB. Telephone: 01984 640688. Email: info@tropiquaria.co.uk

INDEX